Trojan Horse

How the Greeks
Won the Trojan War

Table of Contents

information is without contract or any type of guarantee assurance.

The trademarks that are used are without any consent, and the publication of the trademark is without permission or backing by the trademark owner. All trademarks and brands within this book are for clarifying purposes only and are the owned by the owners themselves, not affiliated with this document.

Introduction

The Trojan War was an epic battle that ended when the Trojan Horse filled with Greeks was received inside the city gates of Troy. This is the summation of what could be history or myth.

According to Homer's Iliad and The Odyssey, the Trojan War was fought because of gods and goddesses, who always liked to play with humans. History tells of something much different. In fact, for several centuries, historians have been trying to prove that Troy actually existed and was not a mythical city.

Until 1871, it was believed the Trojan War was nothing but an epic poem, created by a Greek poet, Homer. It was considered a fictitious account, with no bearing on the real world whatsoever.

Few facts were known prior to 1871, which could be used to determine there was ever such a battle between Greek forces and Trojans protecting their coastal city. It wasn't that war didn't exist or that the Trojans weren't real. It was rather the sparse historical accounts of such an epic war. Plenty of poems and stories based on mythical gods and goddesses were written years after the supposed war, but nothing in the actual history books of the time or since the "Trojan War" lent to the credibility of the story.

Yet, the legend created by Homer continued to plague historians and archeologists. It became a mission for some individuals, including Heinrich Schliemann and Frank Calvert to prove Troy was an actual city that existed in times of antiquity.

Today the question is not about whether Troy existed or did not. It is now fact that there was a city called Troy, where the

Trojans lived, and it was under continued battle against enemy forces.

The real question is—did the Trojan War, as we have come to think of it happen or was it a series of small battles that eventually led to the end of the Trojan people?

Was there, in fact, a Trojan Horse and if so, how did it help win the war for the Greeks?

The focus of the coming chapters, will be to discuss the Trojan Horse as a real concept, not the fictional one from Homer's epic poem. The focus will not be to tell you how Achilles entered the city and helped win the war.

Instead, you will learn who the Trojans were, which Greek faction fought against the Trojans in the last battle, and why the war or series of wars occurred, which led to the innovative concept of the Trojan Horse. In the end, you will also learn the impact the "Trojan Horse" has had on more recent wars. You will discover if the Trojans died out never to be heard of again or if one war ended and more simply occurred.

Chapter 1:
The Bronze Age

Background is needed to answer why the Trojan War occurred and how the Trojan horse was used to win the war. By becoming familiar with the Bronze Age, you can begin to understand the puzzle archeologists are finally starting to uncover.

The Bronze Age is defined by the smelting of copper and tin or by the trading of bronze products. It is also categorized as the third millennium B.C. However, this means different things depending on the regions of the world being discussed.

The Near East, which categorizes the following countries: Anatolia, Elam, Caucasus, Egypt, Mesopotamia, the Levant, and Sistan, were in the Bronze Age from 3300 to 1200 B.C. Later, you should remember that Anatolia was also considered Asia Minor. Anatolia is now called Turkey.

South Asia was said to be in the Bronze Age from 3000 to 1200 B.C. Europe, which includes Aegean began their Bronze Age in 3200 to 600 B.C. Greece was considered as a part of Europe even then, and had a hold on Aegean property, as well as control of the Aegean Sea.

To put these Bronze Age dates into perspective, Greece was a mighty power starting from 1600 B.C. to the end of 1100 B.C.

Note: Many historians trying to prove the existence of Troy, the Trojan War, and the Trojan Horse, believe the Bronze Age ended in 1100 B.C. in Greece and much of the Near East. This will not be debated in this book.

According to the Troia Archeological Site website and UNESCO World Heritage Site, the land considered to be a part of the City of Troy was inhabited from 3000 B.C. to 500 A.D.

The part of this wide range in time period that most concerns us is 1300 to 1000 B.C. It is generally accepted that Homer's Troy and the Troy that fell due to the Greek's Trojan Horse existed sometime between 1300 and 1150 B.C.

Carl Blegen was an archeologist, who worked on the site now considered Troy, between 1932 and 1938. Blegen's chronology of the Troy Strata provides a look at 1300 to 1000 B.C.

Strata is a geological term meaning the layers of earth archeologists have dug up in an attempt to discover historical evidence that will help us understand the ancient civilizations of Troy.

These strata are named by site level: Troy VIh, Troy VIIa, Troy VIIb1, Troy VIIb2, and Troy VIIb3. There is an approximate end date for each site level, meaning the civilization that existed prior to the dates was in some way damaged.

Troy VIh was said to have ended in 1300 B.C. due to an earthquake. Any buildings, people, and artifacts discovered from this time period show a great geological event, such as an earthquake that made people flee and leave everyday items behind.

The next end date for Troy, was 1230-1190/1180 BC, which was Troy VIIa. The listed probably cause was an attack by an enemy. In 1150 BC, Troy VIIb1 was destroyed by an unknown cause. Troy VIIb2 ended in 1100 BC, either due to an earthquake or enemy attack. Troy VIIb3 ended sometime in 1000 BC from an unknown cause.

Troy VIIa is the most important strata. Several archeologists, including Blegen, Schliemann, Calvert, and Strauss accept that the Troy mentioned in the Iliad and Odyssey; therefore, the Troy associated with the war was the Troy VIIa. Blegen has more to support the claim. When digging to the Troy VIIa, he uncovered many unburied skeletons, with Mycenaean Greek arrowheads near the bodies, suggesting the war occurred.

As the discussion deepens about Troy, the Mycenaean Greeks, and the Trojan Horse, remember the probable "Trojan War" was sometime around 1230 to 1180 B.C. This has to do with the unburied skeletons, carbon dating of those skeletons, and the geological evidence that provides a narrowed timeline. The main evidence to suggest this is when the 10 years of war occurred, is a lack of any other cause for the destruction of the city, as well as Homer's account. It also sets a timeline for the information to come in discussing why the war started and how it ended.

Chapter 2:
Who Were the Trojans

Archeologists and historians generally accept that Trojans are a mixture of Anatolian and Luwian origins. This was not always the case. For years, the only evidentiary support that Troy and Trojans existed was Homer's tales. It might seem like the book keeps bringing in Homer and the question of the history versus the myth, but in actuality, to understand the full answer this book is going to provide, you must have a knowledge of the "players."

In Homer's account of the epic war, he used the Greek spelling for names. It seems obvious now that he did so because he was Greek and because when the story was written Greek was a well-known language. To earlier archeologists who were trying to prove the City of Troy existed, there was a 10-year war, and the Greeks won, any information from Homer's epic poems that corresponded to known history was important.

Archeological digs have since answered the question of who the Trojans really were, without any mythological or inaccurate historical assumptions. Archeologists firmly believe the Trojan people were of Anatolian and Luwian decent because of artifacts, buildings, and rituals.

Historical Context Uncovered by Schliemann and Others

Frank Calvert went to what is now Turkey to uncover the true City of Troy. He was not a very well-known archeologist at the time, mostly due to lack of funding and being self-taught. Heinrich Schliemann was largely considered a fraud and discounted for his belief in Troy, but he at least had the funds to make the dig known to the world and to tell the newspapers that he had at last found the real Troy. This occurred in 1871.

What Schliemann considered Troy was little more than a mound of earth, some uncovered bits of pottery, and a deep belief that he was right. Like many in the archeologic and the scientific academia world, proving or discounting a theory is powerful stuff.

Archeologists like Blegen, who arrived in Turkey in 1932, came with the idea of proving Troy existed and uncovered half an acre of the city. It was the citadel. Fast-forward 130 years since Schliemann found his mound, and it is 1988. Strauss and others did their part to uncover a total of 75 acres of city.

In the 1930s, historians postulated that Troy was a mere citadel on the coast of Turkey and not the opulent fortress that the Greeks feared. Yet, 50 years later, with more digging, more strata uncovered, and reaching Troy VIIa, it was known that the city was every bit as large as Homer depicted in his epic tale. It is also at this time, origins of who the Troy descended from were uncovered.

The City Layout, Pottery, and Burials

With the entire city of Troy uncovered by archeologists, work could begin uncovering the Trojans' origins. The city layout represented Anatolian construction. The position of the citadel versus other buildings, including the architecture of those buildings represented the Anatolian culture more so than the Mycenaean Greek culture.

Quite a bit of pottery was uncovered. Again, the majority of the pieces represented an Anatolian connection, where the minority of pieces related more to Greece. Given the shipping lanes for goods coming from Asia through the Aegean Sea and past the strait, where Troy was built, it is not unlikely that traders from Greece sold their pottery in Troy.

Archeological digs uncovered burial grounds, which indicated Anatolian burial practices versus those of the Greeks.

If you add in the location of the city, which was in Anatolia or what is now called Turkey, it would make sense for the Trojans to be descendants of earlier Anatolian people.

There is evidence to suggest a larger Greek population did live in Troy, but this was after the Trojan War is thought to have occurred. This evidence is based on layers of artifacts, in which Greek artifacts were found in strata nearer to the top than Trojan relics.

Where Science Has Yet to Reach

DNA mapping is now possible. More and more species, including human species are being mapped to determine origins. Quite a bit about the skeletons found from prehistoric eras is known thanks to DNA. However, the skeletons found at Troy and thought to have been involved in the Trojan War have yet to undergo DNA profiling, at least that has been released to the public for consumption.

When assessing information for DNA confirmation, it seems scientists have made it as far back as determining the origins of the Etruscans. This is mentioned only to show that the Trojan heritage did not die out completely. DNA evidence shows Etruscan origins relate to the Hittite, and Lydian Kingdoms. Troy was a part of these two kingdoms. More detail about the Hittites will be discussed in chapters about why the Trojan War occurred.

Given the interest in Troy in the academic world, it is likely that DNA profiling of skeletons found at the City of Troy will someday be conducted as a way to answer more questions about the time and the people who lived there.

For now, the simplest answer to who were the Trojans is— Anatolian descendants.

Chapter 3:
The Mycenaean Greeks

In any war there are always at least two parties involved, if not a few other countries because they share alliances with one of the main parties waging war. It might seem a waste of words to discuss who the Greeks were. When discussing the Trojans, there is a question because early assumptions said they were descendants of Greece, when in fact the Trojans displayed more of an Anatolian heritage.

You might even say, "duh they were Greeks." But did you know, there were Mycenaean Greeks and Dorian Greeks living during the Bronze Age? Were you aware that certain cities like Pylos and Athens were populated by Mycenaean Greeks and many of the Dorian Greeks had started to migrate out of Greece, weakening their strong positions as they headed across Europe?

As with many cultures, there are clear divisions, even within a broad term to mean a certain origin. A great example shows that today, labelling someone from Korea as Asian. Yes, Asia as a continent is very large, but it encompasses many cultures, who are diverse in their beliefs, way of life, and language. Chinese is very distinctive from Korean, as is Japanese from the other two languages. Therefore, it is important to know who the Mycenaean Greeks were.

The Mycenaean Period

The Mycenaean period is a time when the Greek mainland was enjoying power and wealth. Their strong holds were Mycenae, Thebes, Tiryns, and Athens. Greek workshops were filled with pottery, bronze, jewelry, carved gems, vases, glass ornaments, and precious metals.

The Mycenaean Greeks had a wide reach for their commerce, sending goods from Greece through the Mediterranean, basically extending from Spain to the Levant. Evidence from this time suggests vases, oil, and wine were the primary goods of trade.

These Greeks were more than traders. They were also warriors and engineers. They created bridges, beehive-shaped tombs, and fortification walls using Cyclopean masonry. The Mycenaean's also established irrigation and drainage systems. Mycenae was viewed as a rich city of gold, while Pylos was sandy (Homer's description). Tablet evidence that were used to record history by scribes, indicated Greece had a very organized feudal system in place. According to Colette Hemingway and Sean Hemingway, the late 1300 century B.C. or 1200s, was a time of decline for the Mycenaean Greeks. The important sites, which had been filled with wealth, suffered destruction, and many Mycenaean's started moving to remote settlements. Pylos, which was the city the king inhabited was destroyed sometime in 1200 B.C. However, it is not completely gone, since it is still a city in Greece and called Pylos-Nestoras today.

Historians consider the complete collapse of the Mycenaean Greeks occurred by the end of 1100 B.C., while many collapses in their cities from 1300 to 1180 B.C. threatened ultimate destruction. It was also a time of rebuilds for parts of the cities the Greeks felt were important.

There is a bit of debate about this time, where some scholars feel it was the population movement that made the Mycenaean's weak. Those who study the Trojan War are more inclined to think it was internal battles, as well as trying to over-stretch their forces to expand and take over cities of shipping importance.

Other Important Players

The world did not consist of just the Trojans and Mycenaean Greeks. There was a lot of strife, natural disasters, and internal wars that started to change existing kingdoms beyond what occurred in Troy and Mycenaean Greek cities.

The Hittites ran a powerful kingdom, which also included Troy. Around the same time Troy fell, Hattusa, the capital of the Hittite Kingdom, was destroyed. Aramaic nomads and Chaldeans were threatening the survival of the Assyrian and Babylonian empires. The Dorian Greeks were migrating and expanding, causing trouble for the Mycenaean Greeks.

It was suggested that the Mycenaean's and Hittites had a peaceful relationship, due to respect and mutual fear of destruction. An accord between Hittite King Hattusili III and King Ahhiyawa of the Mycenaean Greeks existed.

However, Egyptian factions and others like Piyama-Radu constantly moved against the Hittite Kingdom. These two cultures wanted to expand from Africa into Asia, and this was difficult because the Hittite fortress walls were strong. King Ahhiyawa was given Lesbos by Piyama-Radu during the 13th Century B.C. Piyama-Radu even tried to enter Troy as a way to get to the capital of the Hittite Kingdom.

Evidence suggests the relationship with Piyama-Radu was more important to the Greeks than keeping the peace with the Hittite King. Although, for a time after King Hattusili III asked to restore peace, King Ahhiyawa did accept.

Chapter 4:
The Prize is Troy

Examining a map of the world and its countries today, Turkey is north of the Mediterranean Sea. This was Anatolia and during the Trojan War it was a land held by the power of the Hittite Kingdom. Between Greece and Turkey is the Aegean Sea, where the land is split by the Dardanelles, a narrow strait that leads to the Sea of Marmara and then through another strait into the Black Sea. Gaining access to the Black Sea meant trade ships could reach eastern Europe, Russia, and what is now Georgia.

Greece held power in the Mediterranean and Aegean Seas. As a large trade country, with amazing engineering feats, including their ships, it was easy for Greece to control the two seas.

The one thing that stopped Greece from moving east through Asia, was the land on the other side of the Dardanelles, which the citadel of Troy protected.

This land was considered blessed, where water was found in abundance. Clean, drinkable water was imperative and Troy was able to tap into it. The land was also perfect for growing grains and supporting cattle. The seas held plenty of fish to ensure Trojans had plenty of food.

The Trojans were considered middlemen in the shipping industry. The city had little to trade other than textiles and horses. In fact, Troy was known for their exceptionally well bred horses. The city was becoming rich off of controlling travel through the strait and due to the Boreas winds.

For 30 to 60 days in summer the winds would blow making trade easier in the Aegean Sea, through the strait, up the Sea of Marmara and into the Black Sea. When the wind died, ships could not sail because they were not able to tack or go in a zigzag pattern yet.

Ship captains would have to dock at Troy when the winds stopped. It could be for a day or several days that these ships would be moored at Troy. Naturally, it meant trading. Trojans would provide food and lodging to these ships' captains and crew.

Discord over middlemen getting rich was definitely in existence. Greece, of course, wanted the fortress to increase their own riches, as well as to make their way into the Hittite community. Troy was a good place to provide military protection from the west for the Hittite kingdom.

It is clear through various texts, both written history and fictional accounts that Greek perceived Troy as a threat and temptation. Trojans were a threat because they could decide to advance across the strait into Greece and try to sack cities. Troy could also try to take control of the Aegean Sea and become more powerful in the shipping community.

It is clear when examining history, Troy was a prize to win for several opposing forces. Digging through the layers of earth to uncover the history of Troy, it is clear the Trojans faced several skirmishes from the beginning of the Bronze Age till the end of Troy as a city in 500 AD.

It's All About Location and Desire

The predominant theory as to why the Trojan War occurred, either as a 10-year war or several small, intense skirmishes for

10-years, is that Troy was a prized location to the Mycenaean Greeks.

The Greeks desired expansion and control of such a wealthy city. Who needed a middleman getting rich, when it would be better to own the citadel and the city? By owning the city, access to the Hittite Kingdom, Asia Minor and the rest of Asia was easier.

Great leaders and warriors would have thought of this, even as they made living everyday life a priority. The combination of the location of Troy and the desire to be a strong nation that could become richer from controlling the shipping trade would have led to the Mycenaean Greeks developing strategy after strategy to finally sack Troy and end the Trojans.

As the number one reason for why the Trojan War began, was continuously waged, and finally won, was the desire to own the location and make Troy the prize.

Chapter 5:
Homer's Reason for the Trojan War

A battle so epic, it has been recorded in the Iliad, continued in the Odyssey, and written about by different authors for centuries, according to Homer it was started over a woman.

Helen of Troy, a beauty beyond compare, and is said to have started the war between the Mycenaean Greeks and Troy. Helen, according to Homer, was the daughter of Zeus. She was a Greek goddess, wife of Agamemnon, and Prince of Troy's Paris' lover.

The Iliad tells of a diplomatic trip Paris went on to Agamemnon's kingdom in Greece. It is said he was there to bring about a better relationship between Greece and Troy, for trade. In part, many believe he was meant to assure Agamemnon that the Trojans would not rise up against Greece.

The trouble with this tale is that it was an epic poem, written by Homer based on various elements in history, not always taken from 1300 to 1180 B.C. Homer was born centuries after the supposed 10-year Trojan War.

Now we know the Trojan War was at least an event, the debate as to whether it was 10 years in length like the epic battle of Homer's stories or more likely small, intense skirmishes for more than 10 years—is still ongoing.

Scholars of history, archeology, and literature can at least agree that a war or series of wars sacked the city of Troy sometime between 1230 and 1180. More evidence is coming to light in the 1990s and 2000s, suggests the series of battles that eventually ended the Trojans as a people and culture happened between 1200 and 1180 B.C.

We know approximately the when, a general length of the battle, and the where. We also know a bit about the main players, as they were Mycenaean Greeks and Trojans.

Figuring out the direct cause based on literature and what few historical records have been uncovered, is more difficult. Did Helen of Troy actually exist as a real person and not the mythical God, Homer made her out to be? There are no records in Mycenaean Greek or Trojan history that talk of a woman called Helen.

Does this mean she couldn't be real? No, historically women in earlier centuries, including right up until the mid-1900s, were considered an inferior sex. Yes, women could be revered as goddesses, but human females were considered far in-superior to men. If we assume the wife of the current Greek King did exist and she ran off with the Prince of Troy, we could also assume the Greeks were too humiliated at such a wanton act. It can also be assumed that Troy, having ended due to such an act was unable to record the history and just as ashamed of their prince. It is a lot of assuming to do.

A thread of credibility for Homer's Helen of Troy can be found in Hittite records, which mention Akagamunas as the ruler of Ahhiyawa in the 14th century B.C. Based on the spelling and translation into Greek this could refer to Homer's Agamemnon.

Historical Records from Numerous Cultures

There are several cultures nearly from the beginning of the human race that would suggest wars were fought over women.

Kings saw their daughters as sacrifices in marriage to opposing kingdoms. Even in more recent history, the concept of marrying a princess or a royal woman to a prince or king was used to keep peace between two countries. England's history reflects this rather well.

If the princess or royal woman refused, it would be cause for war. It could also be said that the daughter was sent as a peace offering, while a strategy was in place to gain access to the kingdom and take it over with an easier war.

A more relevant concept is the Middle Eastern wars, occurring for the most part due to religious difference. Yes, the "war on terror" is being fought because of 9-11, but there is also a reason relating to "women's rights" and helping women who are suffering or at least not seen to have equal rights. The point is not to debate this current and major fight, but to point out that "women's rights" is bandied about as one reason for military personnel to remain in the Middle East. It gives credibility to the wars being fought with the excuse of a woman or women as the catalyst or a major reason for the fight.

It is very possible that a war could be waged over a woman who ran from her husband to the prince of another country. For now, it is just a theory based primarily on Homer's account of the Trojan War.

If we believe his account as completely, historically accurate, save for the goddess and gods and other mythical elements, then we would need to believe the Trojan War was fought because of one woman's actions and a Trojan prince.

An Excuse to Sack Troy

It is plausible the Mycenaean Greeks used a woman as an excuse to fight the Trojans on their turf. The king of the Mycenaean's could have requested his best warriors take their best ships and start attacking the citadel and attempt to access the city. It would have been a great excuse to fulfil the known desire the Greeks had in wanting Troy and control of the Dardanelles.

The fact that Homer's account makes it a more romantic and tragic tale of a great city coming to its knees in defeat over a woman just makes it a more interesting account of history than the cut and dried version that could have been written.

Will the answer to the question- why did the Trojans fight the Mycenaean Greeks occur and end in defeat for the city of Troy, ever be known? It is unlikely. After 145 years, the answer is still unknown. There are still too many questions and theories being postulated by historians and archeologists because the records are too sparse.

If we assume Homer wrote about a real woman and named her Helen to protect the parties involved centuries later, then we can assume the war's catalyst was this woman.

If we assume there was no woman, then the Greeks found another catalyst to continue pressing the walls of Troy until finally, the Greeks were triumphant over the powerful citadel and the warriors of Troy.

In the end, the reason why the war started is up to you, the reader, to decide knowing both the location as a reason for war and the historical knowledge that women made a great excuse for kings to wage war on other kingdoms.

Chapter 6:
10-Year War or Many Battles?

The Trojan War is considered a ten-year siege on the City of Troy, which ended when the Trojan Horse was rolled into the city, filled with Greeks. However, it may not have been the epic ten-year battle of Homer's epic poems. Does this affect how the war ended—if it was not a ten-year constant siege? Yes, it could definitely affect the validity of the Trojan horse and what was supposedly accomplished with such a Greek creation.

If the validity of Homer's tale is found to be completely false, then it stands to reason, the Trojan horse may be a figment of imagination too. The difficulty historians and archeologists had in believing the Trojan War was actually a real battle comes from the way of life at the time it was said to happen.

There is no doubt that battles occurred with regularity. It doesn't matter whether you look at Egypt, Greece, Troy and the Hittite Kingdom, Ancient China, or any other history of a society and a race of people. War was as common in everyday life as eating.

The basic human instinct to survive, prosper, and find happiness drove societies throughout the known world in the Bronze Age. For a country to survive against another, strength, strategy, and fighting was necessary. It was only the strongest, most prepared who could survive the fights an opponent would start. Fear was certainly a driving force.

Fear that someone else would attack first. Fear of the next opponent being stronger or smarter, or having a better strategy was normal. Women, children, men could not go on with their life each day and think they were totally safe—not like we do today.

When war is half a world away, it is easy to forget that somewhere people are dying in the name of religion, because they made the wrong gesture or said the wrong thing to the wrong, powerful person. In the Bronze Age, it was not possible to forget that death could come during sleep, when awake, or when trying to avoid a fight.

Battles are still continuously waged, even if there is a break in the middle. For a moment consider World War II and Christmas Eve. For one night, both forces, sang and stopped fighting. The next day, the peace was over and fighting began again.

North Korea and South Korea are locked in a battle, where the Demilitarized Zone lay between the border. One country is forever split in two, until something happens to break the tenuous peace.

Already in discussing the Mycenaean Greeks, their relationships and power, as well as that of Troy, you know battles were ongoing. If it was not Egypt trying to break through the Hittite Kingdom and destroy the capital, then it was the Greeks fearing Trojan expansion or vice versa. So there was most certainly war being fought between the Greeks and Trojans, which could have started due to a woman or not.

What one has to figure out is whether that war was non-stop for ten long years or if it was a series of powerful battles that finally ended with the destruction of Troy VIIa.

A Series of Battles is More Likely

As stated, times were hard for those living during the Bronze Age. Unlimited supplies are not something that existed. Travel by ship could take half a year or more because the winds might have stopped for several weeks during the journeys.

Longevity of the people was significantly less due to famine, disease, war, and natural disaster. Population growth, while significant for the time, did not mean there were always enough men to fight a continuous battle.

One small battle, fought with the Trojans sending arrows down into the hearts of Greeks below could have taken out an entire fleet and stopped the war. New warriors would have needed to come to replace the dead, but could Greece spare these warriors to continue the war for ten years?

Greece had other borders, other relationships, and internal struggles to contend with. The reality of the situation is— Greece could not have sustained sending troops year after year, for ten years to try and take over Troy.

It is more likely that attempts were made when Greece felt fear, when a new excuse to fight, or peace in their own land made it possible to try again to end the Trojan society.

That one army, of tens of thousands, continued to attack day in and day out, until the idea of the Trojan horse was formed, is 99% impossible according to most archeologists studying Troy.

Supporting Facts

Back in the chapter about the various strata layers, you learned Troy was destroyed multiple times. Sometimes the city was destroyed because of natural disasters that led to fire and the Trojans abandoning the city, only to come back and build it again.

In between 1300 and ten00 B.C., archeological evidence, is unable to prove a long, never ending war was waged on Troy. The facts show a natural disaster, an attack by an enemy, unknown reasons for destruction, more enemy or natural disaster issues, and more unknown reasons for the city to end.

There is also evidence that sometime between 1200 and 1180, Mycenaean Greeks finally entered the city of Troy, killed numerous Trojans, and left them unburied as they ended a great and powerful city.

The layer of earth on top of this time shows the city was eventually rebuilt, destroyed again and again, with new cities until finally in 500 AD Troy was forever abandoned.

Based on what we know about society and life during 1230 and 1150 B.C. historians can postulate with some accuracy that the siege was a series of battles, with a final brilliant move. The question of whether Troy existed, whether there was at least some type of war, is answered.

Is it like Homer wrote or what many continue to debate as truth—no, not entirely. Proving one theory beyond a reasonable doubt is not possible given the few records that exist about Troy and its end sometime around 1180 B.C.

It would be nice if one opinion or archeological theory proposed by those digging at Troy could be proved true. It would end the debate of what was or could have been. For now, all readers can do, is know that there was war, natural disasters, and Troy were built over and over again, until the city was finally abandoned, forgotten and covered by layers of earth most likely blown around by the Boreas winds so desired by the ship captains of the Bronze Age.

You can choose to believe ten years of constant war occurred each day, until evidence conclusively states otherwise. Ultimately the important point is—the Trojan society written about by Homer was lost. Descendants moved on, a new city was built and new ancestors lived and died on the earth once known to house the grand city of Troy.

Chapter 7:
Greeks Ready for the Fight

The starting point for any information relating to Trojan War is always Homer's sensational epic poem. It might irritate to keep repeating this, but one has to understand to discuss a historical account of the Trojan War, one has to continually refer to the information Homer wrote and any other writers after that. The Aeneid is another tale using the concepts of the Trojan War based on Homer's works. But rather than getting sidetracked on all the books that have been written, it is time to discuss what might have happened during those ten long years in battle.

Assuming it was really ten years, the Greek army had to ready for the battle they would wage from the sea. The Dardanelles strait is 38 miles long and anywhere from 0.75 to 4 miles wide. Today under a mile and up to 4 miles does not seem like a great journey. It can be done in a matter of minutes in the power boats we have today. Ferries, which traverse this area daily do so several times a day.

In antiquity, this was not the case. Greek ships, while advanced, were still under the power of a sail and many men rowing oars in the hold. Historical accounts believe the Bireme, a type of Greek warship, was used in the Trojan War.

It was a long ship, with 30 oars or so on each side, and hundreds of men were needed to power this ship across the sea. The front was shaped in a triangle pattern, with the back turned up to hold the sail in place. It was a longer and narrower ship than the sailboats we are more familiar with today. There was also only one mast, with the sail parallel with the length of the boat, instead of perpendicular.

These ships were made to skim over the water and not to displace a lot of water. In fact, the hulls were flatter than the sail boats that came centuries later. The house had to be flatter, for the ships to move quickly through the water, and even then it could take a great deal of time.

Historical accounts do not state if there was any way from Greece to Troy, other than by ship. While the Greeks did know how to build bridges, there is nothing to suggest they could build an extension bridge about a mile long to go from Greece to what is now Turkey.

Biremes were not made for hauling supplies. They were made for hauling warriors, who had to power the ships across the water. It would have been a tiring prospect. Imagine rowing for days, hoping the wind would help, and eventually reaching Troy.

Only your armada might have been seen or the Trojans could have been expecting it to arrive. Any lookout in the citadel would have known the Greek warships for what they were, since trade ships were much different in shape and size.

Additionally, if the war was started because Paris or whoever the Prince of Troy really was, then Troy would have known to be ready for the Greek army. The situation also occurred in a time, where demands were made. It was about honor to make a demand for a return of a Greek citizen before waging war.

Men had to think about strategy and whether the war could be won, no matter the reason it might have started. Based on this knowledge, it is almost 100% certain the Trojans knew the Greeks were on their way to wage another battle before they arrived on the shores.

The best place for any ships to land was also in the protected harbor, which consistently gained shipping traffic when the winds did not support travel. To moor a ship in other areas would have been difficult, if not near to impossible, and it could have cost the Greek their ships.

It was not as if building a Greek warship could happen overnight or even within a few weeks. It took time to get the wood, mill the wood, and form it into the shape of a ship.

Some accounts believe Trojans would meet the Greeks on the field of battle, spar and then return to their fortress, while the Greeks would go back to their ships. It is a possibility. There were plenty of fields outside of the city walls that could have been used for battles.

If you assess Homer's written work, along with movies like Troy that try to depict the epic battle based on what is known of history, then it is possible a gentlemanly series of wars occurred.

Trojan men could have marched out of the city gates, stood strong and stopped the Greeks from getting inside the city. Trojans could also have stood on the fortress walls, lobbed fire balls, arrows, and hot oil down on the Greeks who were trying to batter their way into the citadel and the city.

Again, it is hard to say with any accuracy and in specific detail, regarding how the war was fought. All that can be said is what is in the books. Homer believed Trojans met on the field of battle, fought, died and kept the Greeks at bay each time.

The Greeks when readying for the war, would have brought some supplies, but not enough to last ten years. Supply ships might have been granted access during times of stalemates or agreed upon rests. Men could not fight day and night, continuously.

If there were even enough men to have several reserve fighters, it would have been difficult to try and battle in the dark hours. In fact, it would be foolhardy of either the Greeks or Trojans to have fought at night.

The armor was not the most comfortable or easiest to move in. Seeing by fire and moon did not mean success would occur. It was generally thought that war should be conducted with honor and strategy.

Surprise attacks such as leading the opposition into a trap was fine, but each needed time to pick up their wounded, their dead, and to pay proper respect to those who had fallen.

Whether the Greeks would return home each time, a battle was waged and lost, is not clear. According to Homer, they stayed near Troy and on Trojan fields. Homer also insists the battles occurred on fields that were often heavy with water, which would have made fighting difficult if not impossible for both parties.

Chapter 8:
Troy was Safe—At Least in Appearances

After what was ten or more years of consistent wars, it seemed like the Greeks had left, at least according to poetical accounts. Homer writes about the Greek ships leaving the harbor after one last battle, apparently knowing they were defeated, and that Troy could not be breached.

Homer also wrote of a present left behind. A relic, icon, or gift for the Trojans, thought to be a sign of peace. Finally, it seemed the Greeks would leave, allow Helen to remain with Paris, and alas peace would return for however long it might last.

Of course, this may not be how it happened at all. The reason many historians tend to agree with Homer's accounting comes down to the Trojan horse. Before getting too comfortable with the topic about the Trojan horse, which is ultimately the discussion to be had as a conclusion regarding the war, it is best to consider whether or not the Trojans would have brought a gift inside the gates of the citadel if the Greeks were still around.

If given a gift, it is natural to assume you would take it. You would not want to insult the person giving the gift and if a ten-year long war occurred, you might be inclined to think the opponent was finally out of strategies or men to continue with the war.

Still, you would be hesitant to accept a gift, particularly, if the entirety of the Greek army was still outside your walls. It would seem more likely in that scenario that the Greeks were waiting for you to fall for the gift, open the doors, and then attack.

The Trojan horse is considered a perfect strategy for sacking a city with few men because it was left as a present and the Greeks retreated. It would be easy for a leader, one tired of war, to think everything was finally over.

It is definitely the greatest strategy in history that the Greeks left and the Trojans fell for such a trick. Being lulled into a false sense of an end to any battle, whether it was the last in a long line of intermittent skirmishes or ten years of fighting, was most definitely the downfall of Troy.

Debating if the Greek Army Actually Left

There are historians who believe the Greek army did not leave. Instead, using something like a battering ram, rather than a Trojan horse, these scholars believe the Greeks finally made it through the gates of the city.

It is a likely scenario, just as likely, in fact, as a Trojan horse being built and left on Troy's doorstep. With continued breaks to recover from various skirmishes, the Greeks could have gone home several times to plan their next attack.

Animals in cages, who are unhappy to be there, will test every inch of their cage to determine any weak points. If a weak point is found after these tests, the animal will use it to escape. The Greeks could have tested and tested for more than ten years to find the weakest point in Troy's fortress, broken through, and sacked the city.

It is difficult to know since the city walls are mostly gone. All that remain of the Troy VIIa that was said to exist during the

Trojan War, are ruins. Like many of the historical records for this time in history, there is little evidence to back up the epic poem Homer created. But what a tale of glory, he wrote.

A city that felt safe, a present filled with Greeks, and the end of a civilization.

Chapter 9:
Is the Trojan Horse Real?

A recent special series on the Trojan War and the horse that ended the war has provided new evidence to the academic world. Archeologists still digging around the city of Troy uncovered what they are calling the real Trojan horse.

These archeologists say they have uncovered several petrified wood pieces that make up the Trojan horse. The curve of the wood, the holes for the nails, and the total number of pieces uncovered are said to form what we have come to think of as the Trojan horse.

It is hard to argue with picture documentation, a PBS special, and archeologists who have worked extremely hard to uncover evidence regarding the Trojan War and the famed horse.

The academic community can; therefore, agree, Troy was not as safe as the Trojans must have thought. The Greeks did, in fact, present a gift filled with Greek soldiers.

But how did the Greek soldiers build such a gift, quickly, and without the Trojans being wary of such a build? Going back to Homer, it is said they built it all in one night using materials from a few of the Greek ships.

It is hard to agree that it would have been built in one night. Building the Trojan horse from boat material is certainly believable. It would have been all they had. If a ship had been destroyed during one of the battles, it is easy to assume it was reassembled into the "gift."

With many Greeks perishing in the war or various battles, it is also likely that the Greek warriors could have used the ships without worrying about the passengers. Less people going home alive would mean less ships could be brought home, after all, the warriors were also the power behind the ship's ability to move.

Before the planks were uncovered inside the citadel, several theories of what the Trojan horse actually was, were posed. Some thought the ships were made with removable pieces that were big enough to hold men, and with a little change in shape they put a horse head and legs on this part of the ship.

Other scholars thought it was nothing but a battering ram, given a special name as such things were in these times. These same scholars thought Homer was mistaken about what the phrase "Trojan horse" meant, so naturally he drew a giant horse, with men inside to depict the coup.

A structure that made legends, the Trojan horse is extremely important to the end of the Trojan civilization. The fact that evidence suggests it is real and was more of a horse shape, with men hiding inside, continues to hold our interest. There has even been some suggestion that the Greeks first thought of building a mallard, so instead of the Trojan horse it would have been the Trojan duck that rolled into the city of Troy and created such an infamous end to an epic battle. This little anecdote is just to show you that no matter what was used, a battering ram, a wooden horse, or a duck—the strategy of the Greeks was brilliant.

It has also helped shape many wars since, but let us not go into that concept yet.

Chapter 10:
The Stealthy Greeks

Inside the Trojan horse were ten brave men, according to Homer. Perhaps, there were more, maybe less. The important element is the strategy. Try as they might for ten years or several decades, the Greeks could not get into the city of Troy and put an end to the Trojan king and his people. Since the earthquake and subsequent rebuild, until sometime around 1180, Troy continued to prosper; Trojans continued to fight battles and win.

It was a time, when the Greeks had to develop a winning strategy or go home defeated yet again. They would have to continue to fear the Trojans would someday take a trip across the Dardanelles in their own warships and attempt to take over Greece.

The Mycenaean Greeks were suffering their own demise and collapse. Pylos was destroyed. More and more people were leaving the main cities due to natural disasters, maybe an illness, and certainly a desire to move on.

The historical accounts show the Mycenaean Greek civilizations, as they were known in the 1300s B.C., were losing the power they had. If something didn't change, they would be at the end of their civilization instead of the Trojans.

With plenty of battles fought and tests on the fortress walls of Troy, it is natural to assume, the Greeks had tried strategy after strategy, until finally coming up with one that will always amaze new civilizations.

We might not understand what the Trojan horse was, although evidence suggests it is exactly as Homer described, but we do know the Greeks were finally stealthy enough to trick the Trojans into letting them into the city.

The unburied skeletons found in the city do exist. There is always the argument that the Mycenaean Greek arrowheads were not related to those skeletons lying in the city streets; however, it seems likely from the oral accounts, poems, and the real Trojan horse that they did enter the city.

It would have been the perfect way for the Greeks to win the war. The Trojans, unsuspecting for the most part, certainly rolled the present into the citadel and were surprised enough by the sudden appearance of Greek warriors to be killed.

What came next is pure conjecture. Had the Trojans simply rolled the present in, leave it unattended save for a few warriors and go about their day? Is it possible that they were partying since the Greeks were gone? They might simply have been enjoying a meal when the Greeks made their way out of the horse for their surprise attack.

It would make sense that most of the Trojan warriors were not around the gift. Perhaps a few were guarding it to ensure nothing untold happened and they were overpowered by the Greeks coming out of the horse.

It seems highly likely that after any guards were killed that the Greeks would open the door to their fellow warriors. It would make more sense for the entire Greek army that was in the vicinity to have sailed back in the night, moored at the docks, made their way to the closed fortress gates, and helped sack the city.

Warfare at the time was nothing like it is now, in terms of the weapons or technology. Seeing at night would have been difficult. Killing with anything other than fire, swords, and arrows were less likely, certainly guns did not exist then. The more warriors let into the city, the easier it would be to suddenly end the fight.

The theory that if you kill the leader and all opposition stops is not truly how a war would end, even then. Battles at this time were about chivalry. It was one on one combat, bows and arrows, and sword fights. At the end of the day, the war was placed on hold for the wounded to be attended and men to prepare for the next battle.

Trojans would have been angered over the coup and certainly upset at the humiliation the deception caused. It was also a time when slaves were taken. Any surviving Trojans may well have been taken captive and made to work for the Greeks.

Since we cannot picture the entire battle, and can only assume what happened, it is up to you to decide if the entire Greek army entered the city that night. From a military standpoint, it makes sense for the Greeks to wait in a place on their ships that the Trojans would not be able to see. It also makes sense that their ships would have continued traveling back to Greece for a short time, until darkness fell and then for the Greeks to turn their ships back around in time for a predetermined time to meet their fellow warriors inside the city.

The element that is most important regarding the deception, is in truth the deception rather than what happened once the horse was inside. Certainly, if the coup had failed and the Greeks died inside the horse, the strategy and deception that became a part of later wars may not have happened in exactly the same way.

It is because the plan worked that history was forever changed in how to fight battles. Chivalry, heroes, and the gentlemanly fights on the battle fields that always ended for supper time didn't immediately change. But certain things did.

Chapter 11:
Getting into the City was the Battle

It is clear that forces attempted to get into Troy and destroy the middlemen. The Trojans were a civilization to fear only because they owned land that protected the coastal region for the Hittite Kingdom. The Hittites had plenty of enemies and they were Trojan allies.

Piecing together historical records and accounts, it is clear that war was a constant part of life. It is also clear that Troy or a city of a different name, was rebuilt time and again on the site, known as Hissarlik, in some of the texts.

Any of the known accounts of the time between 1300 B.C. and 1000 B.C. make it clear that Troy was a fortress that was hard to get into. One event is clearly considered the Trojan War, where the enemy attacked and the city was destroyed. Other endings to the cities built on that same site occurred due to natural disasters. It needs to be mentioned again that some destruction that occurred is unknown at this point.

The point in all of these statements—is the Greek army needed to get into the city. Homer and all other information says it was extremely difficult for the Greeks to breach the fortress walls and get into the city. These same accounts make it seem impossible for the Greeks to reach the king of Troy and put an end to him.

It could be debated all day and for centuries, and it certainly has that the reason the Greeks were so interested in Troy was their alliance with the Hittites and the location of this trade city to protecting the Hittite Kingdom.

An important factor is that the Greeks came up with the Trojan horse as a way to finally get into the city. More than half the battle, the Greeks faced was in ensuring they got through the tough walls and could reach the Trojan warriors to end them completely.

The Trojan horse is just the vessel that made this happen. No matter what tool was used, the fact that it worked, is how the course of history was changed for the Trojans.

The battle was pretty much over once the Greeks entered the city. It would have been difficult for the Trojan warriors to win, unless they were smart enough to wait for the surprise attack. We know the Trojans were caught by surprise, killed, and the city destroyed, thus they were not smart enough to see through the attack allowing the battle to be won as soon as they rolled the horse into their city.

Yes, obviously, there was still fighting that needed to occur. The Trojan warriors had to die or at least be submissive and accept the defeat. However, without the Trojan horse allowing entry into the city this would not have been the case.

It would be like someone consistently knocking on the door, asking for entry, and rebuffed time and again. Consider for a moment the ploys used by some famous serial killers, who killed their victims in their homes. These victims were lured by a ploy, one that seemed innocent and not harmful at all. In walks the intruder and death is a result.

Yet, if the victim denied entry, called the police, and remained safe inside where the killer could not get to them, their life would not have ended. In this context, it makes it clear that had the Trojans not allowed the Greeks in under the guise of a gift, the city might have lasted for a few more years, several more decades, or become an even greater power.

We might say the same thing of the Trojans. The Trojans unaware of the dangers lurking in the belly of a horse, let in the opposition and it was the end of the battle. All the Greeks had to do was find all the warriors, fight, wound or kill, and the city was theirs.

Chapter 12:
A Horse of a Different Color

Sorry for the play on words in the chapter title, but it was hard to resist. The Trojan War or series of wars could have ended much differently for the Trojans. Even according to Homer, had the Trojans followed the advice of certain characters, the coup would not have worked.

A strategy that we take as very simple in today's time, was magnificent in its simplicity to the point that it actually worked. It was unheard of for any real strategy to be a part of the battles waged during the Bronze Age. It was more about men going out, finding an opponent and seeing who might be killed or at least wounded. It was about making sure opponents could not return to the battlefield, more than deception and strategy.

If strategic warfare had been more common, then the horse that ended the Trojans in approximately 1180 B.C. may never have been an issue. Yes, Homer is fiction and a mythic, epic poem, but there is every chance some leader, warrior, or part of the royal party would have said burn the horse and don't you "dare bringing it inside the gates."

How would history be different if the horse never made it into the city of Troy? What if the Trojans were smart enough to recognize that the Greeks were trying one last ploy before really returning home, defeated?

For one thing, we would not be some enamored of the Trojan horse as a tool in the war. It might have taken well beyond the 5th century B.C. for similar deception strategies and strategic warfare to be considered. Then again, things might have happened the same way, only with one key difference. The Trojans would have been the winners of that battle instead of the Greeks.

It is easy to imagine that the Trojans would have been raising their weapons and cups in joy to show they did not fall for the ploy and then turn around and try to come up with a better strategy had they not seen their demise.

The Trojans could have very easily burned the horse and all of the Greeks inside. What made them bring the horse into the city instead?

For one, it could have been the way the war was waged at the time. Another reason is pride. The Greek ships were gone. They left a present as a peace offering, or so it appeared. Cheering that the war was over and the Greeks were beaten would have been easier than to worry about possible traps.

What if the Trojans had survived that skirmish? By all accounts, Troy was rebuilt a few more times, even with the fall of the "Greatest" Trojans. It could be argued that the fate of the Trojans was to die out, whether it happened in 1180 B.C. or in 500 A.D.

Another possible earthquake and attack did in another city, built on top of Troy. An unknown caused ended it a few times, so what or who is to say that Troy wouldn't have ended by another opponent in a similar way?

It is impossible to rewrite history. The Trojans of Homer's imagination scattered or died when the city was sacked by the Mycenaean Greeks. The Mycenaean Greeks didn't survive much longer either. In the end, other civilizations have started and stopped.

Today, people live in Turkey. The once grand city of Troy is a 75-acre dig site being excavated for knowledge, and we have air travel for better trade. Civilizations will continue to come and go. Advancements in human knowledge, technology, and various industries will continue.

But there is one thing that will remain a part of history forever—The Trojan horse and its meaning to later warfare. It is not a matter of whether the Trojan War occurred in ten years or a hundred. It is not that the Greeks won, it is how they won by using deception and a "horse" that make the history of the Trojans and Greeks important enough to write and read about.

Chapter 13:
The Impact the Trojan Horse Created

Homer took the information he learned about the Trojan War and wrote two epic poems. Historians cannot even agree on when he lived. Some believe he was born sometime in 1200 B.C. Others feel it is more likely that he was alive sometime in the 8th century B.C. For the most part the consensus is that Homer lived at least 400 years after the Trojan War took place.

Dating the poems is based on certain things mentioned about historical events that took place. Many believe Homer used wars prior to the Trojan War and after to create his tale. Homer was also not mentioned until around the 8th Century B.C. in historical texts.

The point is—the Trojan horse had an impact even after Troy VIIa fell because of the Greeks' deception. Without a written account that would interest listeners and readers, the Trojan horse might have fallen away into history, never to be known.

It is due to the Iliad and Odyssey, as well as other works that transcended time that numerous civilizations are aware of the Trojan War, the use of the Trojan horse, and the end of a once great city.

In the 5th century B.C., Sun Tzu wrote *The Art of War*. It became *the* military strategy guide for strategic warfare. The precepts he wrote about helped Asian armies fight amazing wars. But one has to ask, would Sun Tzu have come up with some of these concepts without the Trojan horse? Maybe, it would take a deeper look into how far the Iliad and other Trojan War stories travelled, but the fact remains the Trojan horse had a significant impact on how wars were fought in Asia Minor and later on.

Even today, the simplicity of the Trojan horse is considered in certain circumstances, albeit a different version, but nevertheless similar concepts are used. If you think about it, military personnel going in during the night to try and capture an enemy, dates back to the time when the Trojan horse was used.

Archeological Impact

It is not just about the way war might have changed and did change after the tale of the Trojan horse made its way around the world—it is also archeology. Numerous archeologists have spent countless hours searching for and digging up Troy. These many people dug and dug until they found Troy VIIa. These same archeologists have worked to find corresponding texts, written and oral evidence, and artifacts that can confirm the Trojan war happened and the Trojan horse was as glorious an end to the Trojan civilization as Homer made it out to be.

We are still trying to determine the truth of the war. Many still create pictures and TV shows to share their theory of what happened, as well as the evidence to back it up. Historical writers read through various material, visit the site, and attempt to discuss the Trojan War and how the Trojan horse ended a ten-year or longer battle.

The Trojan horse as a war strategy interests us. We can't help, but try to find the answers. Simply put, the war happened either due to a woman or due to the location of Troy and the fear the Greeks felt.

The war was fought as any war during that time, until one or more intelligent Mycenaean Greek warriors came up with the strategy to use the Trojan horse to completely annihilate the Trojans.

Chapter 14:
The Trojans Lived, Weakened Perhaps

Homer made it sound like the heroes who helped the Greek, made their way home and the Trojans were a forgotten people. We know that Troy rose again. It was not just a city of Greeks once it was rebuilt. Perhaps the Greeks gave up wanting the city or maybe they couldn't hold onto it as their own demise began in earnest.

Those who lived in Troy VIIb1 through VIIb3, could well have been descendants of the Trojans who perished in the Trojan War. It is clear that some part of their DNA remains given the Etruscan connection.

While Homer's Trojans were completely annihilated and wiped off the map, the real truth is a part of them still live on in the descendants that remain, even if the blood is diluted numerous times over.

Like the Romans, who rose to power later on, it is possible that the Trojan warriors were kept as slaves, at least those who did not die in the war. It is also possible that the woman of Troy became wives to Greek husbands, and continued a nomadic existence as the Mycenaean Greeks fell from power and started moving to refugee locations.

Others most likely returned to the city they knew after it was clear the Greeks or whoever rebuilt the city would not kill them on sight.

A lesson that can be learned here is that while wars are fought in the moment of history, when it ends and when a civilization ends or changes into a new group, a war waged may no longer be of importance for millennia.

Look at how long it took for us to uncover the truth about the Trojan War. It was not until 145 years ago we took the Trojan War as true history. The Trojan horse was considered a fictional concept until the planks of what are most likely the Trojan remains were found.

Only the lesson that allowing a gift passed your fortress walls, the gate to your home, or through your front door is what is really most important. Without that lesson things might have been different. We might not remember to be careful, when a stranger approaches. It is very possible that we may never have considered the dangers of a mundane object as dangerous, at least not in the context that we do today.

So the Trojans live, whether in our DNA or because of the lesson their error has taught us. In one day, when the Trojans found the horse, their lives as they knew them ended and the Trojan War or various wars ended for at least a little while, until the city was built again.

Conclusion

Thank you for purchasing this book!

I hope this book was able to help you understand the historical aspects of the Trojan War, the part the Trojan horse played in that war, and how the demise of a society occurred.

Hopefully, you found a little pleasure in reading about these long ago times, with these long ago warriors who may have fought over a woman or simply wanted to protect what they felt was important.

The Trojan horse, whether real or of Homer's imagination, has definitely left an impact on the world, including one on today's world. An innovative concept that a war could be won with a gift of hidden soldiers is and always will be considered one of the greatest feats of history. Certainly the strategy and intelligence behind such a concept is one that makes you reconsider all war strategies.

Finally, if you enjoyed this book, please take the time to share your thoughts and post a review on Amazon. It would be greatly appreciated!

Thank you and good luck!

Preview of
Greek Gods by Patrick Auerbach

Introduction

Greek mythology is deeply ingrained in our culture. References to it are everywhere. In psychology we have the Oedipus complex and the opposition of Apollonian and Dionysian temperaments. In popular speech we describe epic journeys as odysseys, speak of other people 'opening Pandora's box' or 'having the golden touch,' and describe certain types of computer malware as 'Trojan horses.' Western literature and drama, of course, owe a deep debt to the Greek myths. Eugene O'Neill's Mourning Becomes Electra and Sartre's The Flies are two very different reinterpretations of the story of Orestes and Electra. Paul Frazer's Civil War novel Cold Mountain draws heavily on the Odyssey. Cocteau's Orphee, Rilke's Sonnets to Orpheus and Tennessee Williams' Orpheus Descending are all drawn from the same myth cycle.

It's difficult to draw up one comprehensive account of Greek mythology. Greek creation stories and accounts of the gods are many, varied and contradictory. Cultural understandings and religious practices changed, and the sacred stories shifted with them. When the Roman empire conquered the Greek lands they took over the Greek pantheon, renamed all the deities, and added in some stories of their own. What follows is an introduction to some of the common understandings of the gods and to some of the great cosmic and human stories that have left an enduring mark on our culture. Further reading suggestions are in the 'Sources' section at the end.

Chapter One:
The Creation and the Gods

In The Beginning...

How did the world begin? The stories vary widely. One common feature is that the gods who reigned on Mount Olympus, the gods featured in the legends and the worship of the time, were the world's children, not its creators. In the beginning was chaos. From this chaos the first divine beings arose, and from their couplings life and order filled the void. But there was still plenty of chaos to go around. The ancient gods made war on each other, and there was great destruction before the Olympian gods arose and the world gained a precarious stability. Even the Olympians were hardly of one mind, and the wars of men were complicated, sometimes determined, by the power-struggles of the gods.

The Olympian creation myth, which was at some point the canonical version, says that in the beginning Gaia, the Earth, emerged from Chaos and, in her sleep, bore a son, Uranus, who ascended to the mountaintops and showered her with fertile rain; she conceived and bore other children--plants, beasts, birds, fish, one-eyed Cyclopes, hundred-handed Hecatoncheires, and also the Titans, the vast and powerful ancestors of the Olympian gods.

Uranus, wishing to maintain control of the world, imprisoned the Cyclopes and Hecatoncheires in the dark depths of Tartarus, far below the earth. Gaia was furious and encouraged the Titans, who were still free, to attack Uranus. Cronus, the boldest of them, did so, castrating him. Uranus either died or fled, predicting that Cronus also would be overthrown by his children. The splashing foam produced by

51

Uranus' genitals and Cronus' sickle falling into the sea engendered Aphrodite (Venus to the Romans), the goddess of love; Uranus' blood falling on the land brought forth the nymphs, the giants, and also the Furies, who punish mortals who kill or injure their relatives.

Cronus, victorious, did not release the prisoners from Tartarus. He married his sister Rhea and set himself up as ruler of the world. To prevent Uranus' prophecy from coming true he swallowed all the children Rhea bore him; but when she bore Zeus she gave the child to Gaia to hide, and gave her husband a stone to swallow. Zeus was raised in secret. As he grew to maturity he asked the Titaness Metis to help him defeat his father and revive his siblings. Metis gave Cronus a potion that made him vomit forth his children, who promptly joined Zeus in making war on the Titans. After a ten-year struggle, Gaia urged Zeus to free the Cyclopes and Hecatoncheires, who would prove formidable allies; Zeus did so, and they armed him with the thunderbolt, also giving powerful weapons to his brother gods. Cronus and the other male Titans were then banished to Tartarus, promising that Zeus also would be overthrown by one of his sons. Atlas, who had led the Titans in war, was punished by being forced to hold up the world. Metis and the Titanesses remained free, as did the Titans Prometheus and Epimetheus, who had taken joined with the Olympians before the end.

The Olympian Gods (and a few others)

The Olympian gods, and the Titans who were left to rule with them, were the great supernatural figures in the foreground of the myths. However, they were not all-powerful. Their destinies as well as those of mortals were determined by the Moirae or Fates, three women who worked together on a tapestry whose threads were the lives of all living things. Their ancestry was unknown and their workings were mysterious, even to the gods.

Gods:

Zeus (called Jupiter or Jove by the Romans) was the greatest of the Olympian gods, ruler of the skies and wielder of the thunderbolt. His power was great but not infinite, and he could be deceived. He could also be deceitful--though married to Hera, he had frequent affairs with attractive goddesses, nymphs and mortal women, which he tried (usually unsuccessfully) to conceal from his wife. He expected righteous behavior from humans--oath-keeping, respect for the dead, and kindness to beggars and strangers.

Poseidon (Neptune to the Romans), brother of Zeus,was second greatest of the gods, the ruler of the sea, creator of horses, and wielder of an immensely powerful trident made for him by the Cyclopes.

Hades, (Pluto to the Romans), brother of Zeus, was the ruler of the underworld (named Hades after him) and the dead. He had a helmet of invisibility given to him by the Cyclopes.

Apollo, son of Zeus and the Titan Leto, twin brother of Artemis, was the god of the sun, the arts, and prophecy. He could not lie. His oracle at Delphi gave true answers to every question, although sometimes the truth was stated so mysteriously that the questioner went home no wiser. He also gave the gift of prophecy to Cassandra, a mortal woman, princess of Troy, when he was courting her; when she refused him, he couldn't take the gift back, but he added the curse that her prophecies would never be believed. Apollo was also the protector of herdsmen and shepherds and the father of Asclepius, the god of healing.

Dionysus (Bacchus to the Romans), son of Zeus and either Demeter or Semele depending on which myth you read, was the god of wine, fertility, ecstasy, madness, and the theater. His death and rebirth are associated with the changes of the seasons. He gave grapes to humans and taught the art of wine-making. Dionysus sometimes granted dangerous wishes to mortals. He offered King Midas anything he wanted, and Midas asked to have everything he touched turn to gold. Dionysus granted the wish and watched while the king's food and drink turned to gold as he touched them, while his dearly loved daughter went to comfort him and turned to gold as she embraced him. Then Dionysus had pity on the king, restored the girl to life and and took the gift back.

Eros (Cupid to the Romans) was the god of love and desire. In some stories he is one of the first gods to arise from chaos; in others he is the son of Aphrodite, by either her husband Hephaestus or her lover Ares. Eros' arrows, often shot at random, caused mortals and immortals who were struck by them to fall in love. Eros himself fell in love with Psyche; their story is told below.

Ares (Mars to the Romans), son of Zeus and Hera, was the god of war in general (as opposed to defensive war, Athena's specialty). Many of the Greeks looked down on him as bloodthirsty and mindless; many of the Romans looked up to him as valiant and glorious.

Hermes (Mercury to the Romans), whose father was Zeus and whose mother was Atlas' daughter Maia, was the god of thieves and of commerce; as a day-old child he stole Apollo's cattle and, when Apollo came to reclaim them, got Apollo to leave them with him in exchange for the lyre, which he had just invented and was willing to trade away. Hermes also carried messages for Zeus and guided souls to the world of the dead. Pan, the god of shepherds, was Hermes' son.

Hephaestus (Vulcan to the Romans), son of Hera--some say hers only, some say hers by Zeus--was the smith to the gods, maker of their weapons and also of the lovely things which adorn Mount Olympus. He was crippled, having been thrown down from Olympus either by Hera (who was disappointed by his ugliness) or by Zeus (who was angry with him for standing up for his mother); but after his fall he was loved and honored by the Olympians. He was also honored by humans, to whom he taught metalwork and other necessary crafts. He was a gentle and peace-loving god. In many stories he was married to Aphrodite, though she was enamored of Ares and had an affair with him.

Prometheus was one of the Titans who survived into the age of the Olympian gods. In some stories he helped Athena to emerge from the head of Zeus. He was the maker and protector of humanity, at great cost to himself; he became the god of science. More of his story is told in "Prometheus, Epimetheus and Pandora" below.

Goddesses:

Hera, (Juno to the Romans), wife and sister of Zeus, was the protector of married women and mothers. Most of the stories about her describe her jealousy of Zeus and her revenges on his paramours.

Athena (Minerva to the Romans), who sprang full-fledged from the head of Zeus rather than being born in the usual way, was the goddess of wisdom and of defensive war (in most accounts--though in the Iliad she's described as being on the side of the Greek attackers of Troy.). Poseidon created horses, but Athena tamed them. She taught mortals to plow and raise crops and tame animals, she created the first olive tree, and she invented pottery, weaving and spinning. She could also be vindictive. When a mortal woman named Arachne claimed that she could weave as well as Athena, and actually challenged her to a weaving contest where she wove as skillfully as Athena (showing scenes of the Gods behaving foolishly, whereas Athena's tapestry showed the Gods in their glory), Athena destroyed Arachne's web and struck her with fear and shame so that she hanged herself. Athena pitied her then and brought her back to life as a spider. Our word 'arachnid' comes from Arachne's name.

Aphrodite (Venus to the Romans), born of the foam of the sea, was the goddess of love, supremely beautiful and the giver of joy. She could also be cruel, deceiving men and driving them to despair. In most myths her husband is Hephaestus and her lover is Ares.

Artemis (Diana to the Romans), daughter of Zeus and Leto and twin sister of Apollo, was the virgin goddess of the hunt, wilderness and wild creatures, virginity, childbirth and children. In later stories she is said to be the same as Selene, goddess of the moon, and Hecate, goddess of the underworld.

Demeter (Ceres to the Romans), sister of Zeus, was the goddess of the harvest and the earth's fertility. Athena taught men to plow, but Demeter gave them grain, and Demeter caused all growth. Demeter's beautiful daughter, Persephone (Proserpina to the Romans), was abducted by Hades; Demeter, who hadn't seen what happened, searched for her for a long time, grieving, and her grief stopped life and growth. Zeus, wishing the world to live, ordered Hades to send

Persephone back; but Persephone had eaten in the Underworld and could not leave it forever. For four months of the year she was bound to return to Hades, and once again Demeter grieved and growth was halted, but for the remainder of the year Persephone was with her mother and all green things grew and thrived. According to some stories Dionysus is Demeter's son.

Hestia (Vesta to the Romans), sister of Zeus, was the virgin goddess of home and hearth.

Click here to check out the rest of Greek Gods on Amazon.com

Or go to: **Amazon UK Link** (if you live in the United Kingdom)

Printed in Great Britain
by Amazon